THROUGH THE WINDOW

VIEWS OF MARC CHAGALL'S LIFE AND ART

BY
BARB ROSENSTOCK

ILLUSTRATED BY
MARY GRANDPRÉ

ALFRED A. KNOPF 🐕 NEW YORK

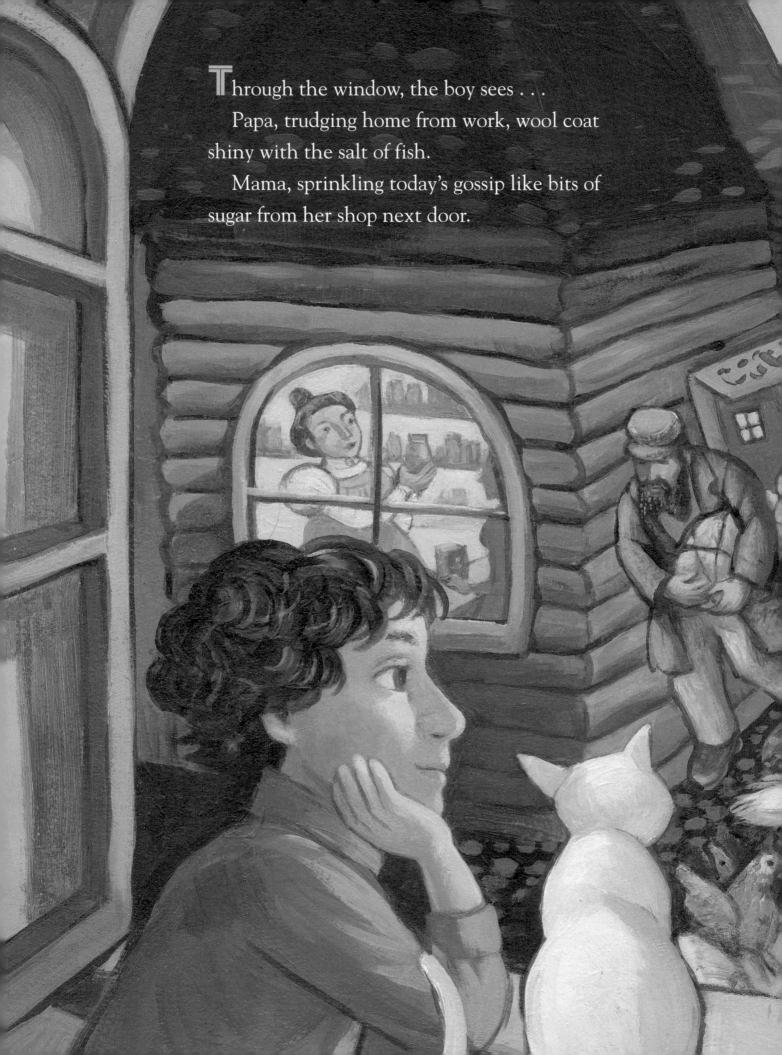

Through the window, the boy sees . . .

Papa, trudging home from work, wool coat
shiny with the salt of fish.

Mama, sprinkling today's gossip like bits of
sugar from her shop next door.

A parade of plodding oxen, wandering goats, and flapping hens.

Neighbors squabble, rabbis bless, a bowlegged fiddler plays on a rooftop.

His own reflection, blue-eyed, curly-headed, Moishe Shagal, daydreaming in Vitebsk, his hard-life city, full of hugs.

Through the window, the student sees . . .
His future—butcher, baker, blacksmith—but turns away.
A classmate sketching a face from a book. His mind blossoms.

The power of pictures. He draws and erases, dreams in color while Papa worries.

A folder of pages laid on an art teacher's desk. Mama asks,

Does this boy have talent?

Pursed lips, a shrug, then a nod, and a new artist is welcomed.

His brave heart flying through the streets,

on a journey unknowable.

Through the window, the misfit sees . . .

Two-faced slivers of St. Petersburg, glittering city of czars and princes, neighbors crammed in filthy rooms, Russia's poor, ignored.

Successful students copy ancient Greeks trapped in faded plaster.
Stale professors dismiss his easel flooded with fragments of folktales.

The store signs he paints to keep from starving sway,
their marching letters blur and whisper, "Move on."

Through the window, the painter sees . . .
The magic of Paris: Eiffel's tower, latticed galleries,
Cézanne, Gauguin, Matisse.

His name transformed to Marc Chagall, French, elegant, light as pâtisserie.

New friends: poets peeling pears, Cubists clinking cups—toasting this good-life city.

New colors: acid yellow, blazing orange, chrome green, blue in all its languages.

The world tilting, soldiers replace artists in the cafés.

Home, for a sister's wedding, he's stranded as the world wars, tangled in darkness.

Through the window, the revolutionary sees . . .
The hope of Russia's riches spread equally among its people.
Bella—wife, mother, and model; gentle kisses softening
these lean years.

Leaders wrestle for power, crushing freedoms in life and art.
Restless crowds controlled through muscular portraits.
His radical canvases, orange faces, sky-blue horses,
called harmful, hated.

He packs his imagination, leaves Russia,
and turns back to the City of Light.

Through the window, the master sees . . .

His prized paintings grown famous around the world.

A misty woman on a parti-colored rooster. Frilly acrobats tumble in the sky.

Spirited rabbis, milkmaids, and fiddlers float through his plush studio.

Again, war stomps across France. He escapes to America, crosses the ocean like a flaming dove.

New materials: clay, fabric, tiles, stone, metal, glass.

He starts over again, and again,
the way art has forever been made.

Through the window,

the old man sees . . .

A rippling kaleidoscope of magic memories.

His dreams, real and imagined,

broken apart and fit back together.

A crowd of artisans firing, tracing, cutting, and wrapping.
Small water-colored cartoons transformed into vast walls of art.

Like a child, he dabs and smudges each pane,
leaving his peaceful mark in places to heal, pray,
and learn.

Through Marc's windows, we see . . .
Laughing mothers, tired fathers, musicians keeping
time for animals on parade.
Characters we know deep inside, though we've
never met.
Marching letters whispering secret truths
through the glass.

Blue, blue, forever blue, breathtaking oceans of flashing spirit.
Children's faces tangled in rainbows, playing with light, watching our hard-life, good-life world, full of hugs.

AUTHOR'S NOTE

The artist Marc Chagall was born Moishe Shagal on July 7, 1887, to a Jewish family in Vitebsk, Belarus, which was then part of the Russian Empire. From his earliest years, he was fascinated by views glimpsed through windows. He often sketched and painted windows, flung open or shut tight, neat and square, twisted and bent, some filled with welcoming light, others dark and threatening. He posed his sister, brother, wife, daughter, friends, strangers, imagined characters, and himself all in front of windows.

Chagall's window paintings often show the many places he lived. He painted views from windows in his hometown (*View from a Window [Vitebsk]*, 1908) and scenes from his childhood. During the winter of 1906–1907, he left Belarus to study art in St. Petersburg. At that time there were many restrictions on where Jews could study, travel, and live. Chagall painted village windows as part of *The Wedding* (*Russian Wedding*) from 1909, one of the few paintings that survive from those years. Moishe's failure to find artistic success in Russia as well as anti-Semitic sentiment led him to move to Paris in 1910.

There, the young artist changed his name to its French form, Marc Chagall. He visited city museums and galleries, met avant-garde poets and painters experimenting with new forms of art. His unique style developed, featuring bright, saturated colors, and dreamlike images, many with Russian-Jewish subjects. A famous painting from that time is the Cubist-influenced view from his apartment, *Paris Through the Window*. Chagall exhibited in Paris salons and had his first solo exhibit in Berlin in 1914.

While Chagall was visiting Vitebsk for a sister's wedding, World War I broke out and he was unable to return to Paris. He settled in his hometown and married Bella Rosenfeld in 1915. Their daughter, Ida, was born the following year. Chagall supported the political revolutions that transformed Russia into the Soviet Union. He was appointed director of an art school. After conflicts with other school officials, Chagall moved to Moscow to design and paint sets for its Jewish Theatre. A view from his *dacha*, or cottage, outside Moscow can be seen in *Window at the Dacha*.

Disillusioned with the Soviet system, Chagall obtained a precious travel visa in 1922. Chagall discovered his early paintings had become famous, and that friends had tried and failed to reach him in the eight years he'd lived in the Soviet Union. While waiting to return to France, he wrote his poetic autobiography, *My Life*, on which the rhythms of this book's language are based. In 1923,

America Windows, 1977. 244 x 978 cm. Art Institute of Chicago.

"FRANCE IS MY REAL HOME."
—MARC CHAGALL

The Birthday, 1915. 31¼ x 39¼ in. Museum of Modern Art.

Chagall settled in Paris. His art sold well, and the family lived comfortably there for eighteen years. Paintings from this time featuring windows are *Celebration in the Village* and *The Pink Chair*, among many others. In 1941, Chagall and his family fled occupied France during the World War II Nazi persecution of Jews and other minorities.

They found asylum in the United States, where Chagall continued his career. After a sudden illness in 1944, Bella died in a New York hospital. Heartbroken, Chagall stopped working for nine months. His painting *Hommage au Passé* (*Honor the Past*) portrays a painter near a window with his memories of a woman. He started work again by designing sets and costumes for a New York City Ballet production of Stravinsky's *Firebird*. In 1948, Chagall returned to Paris permanently. There, he worked on ceramics,

"FOR ME A STAINED-GLASS WINDOW IS A TRANSPARENT PARTITION
BETWEEN MY HEART AND THE HEART OF THE WORLD." —MARC CHAGALL

The Green Violinist, 1923–24. 78 x 42¾ in.
Solomon R. Guggenheim Museum.

stone sculptures, mosaics, and tapestries, in addition to painting.

In his late sixties, Chagall took up a new artistic challenge and learned the art of making stained-glass windows. He designed his first original window at the age of seventy. In 1958, Chagall began creating windows in collaboration with the famous glassworker Charles Marq and his team of French craftsmen. Chagall designed over fifty windows in both Europe and the United States. The most well-known are a set of twelve windows (*The Twelve Tribes of Israel*) for Hadassah–Hebrew University Medical Center in Jerusalem, the *Peace* window for the United Nations Headquarters in New York, three windows for Saint-Stephen Cathedral in Metz, France, and three *America* windows at the Art Institute of Chicago. I saw the *America* windows about a year after their 1977 installation and will remember forever walking down a set of stairs to be enveloped in the warmth of Chagall's brilliant blue light for the first time. Marc Chagall drew his last window design at the age of ninety and continued working on existing window commissions until he died on March 28, 1985, at the age of ninety-seven, at home in his sleep. I imagine he was dreaming.

"IN OUR LIFE THERE IS A SINGLE COLOR, AS ON AN ARTIST'S PALETTE,
WHICH PROVIDES THE MEANING OF LIFE AND ART. IT IS THE COLOR OF LOVE."
—MARC CHAGALL

SOURCES

Art Institute of Chicago. *America Windows*. artic.edu/
exhibition/Chagall

Art Institute of Chicago. *America Windows*, video. youtube
.com/watch?feature=player_embedded&v=Bz2mioCp-M0

Artists of the 20th Century. *Marc Chagall*, DVD. New Jersey:
Kultur International Films, 2004.

Baal-Teshuva, Jacob. *Marc Chagall: 1887–1985*. Cologne,
Germany: Taschen, 2008.

British Pathé. *Marc Chagall Works on a Series of Stained Glass*,
video. britishpathe.com/video/marc-chagall-works-on-a-
series-of-stained-glass-wi/query/Staines

Chagall, Bella. *First Encounter*. New York: Schocken, 1987.

Chagall, Marc. *My Life*. New York: Da Capo Press, 1994
edition.

Chagall, Marc, and Jose Maria Faerna (ed.). *Chagall*.
New York: Abrams, 1995.

Freund, Miriam. *Jewels for a Crown: The Story of the Chagall
Windows*. New York: McGraw-Hill, 1962.

Greenfeld, Howard. *The Essential Marc Chagall*. New York:
Abrams, 2002.

Harshav, Benjamin. *Marc Chagall and His Times:
A Documentary Narrative*. Stanford, CA: Stanford
University Press, 2003.

Marteau, Robert. *Stained Glass Windows of Chagall*,
1957–1970. New York: Tudor, 1973.

Olin, Chuck. *A Palette of Glass*, video. New York: Phoenix
Films, 1977.

Walther, Ingo F., and Rainer Metzger. *Marc Chagall,
1887–1985: Painting as Poetry*. Cologne, Germany: Taschen,
2006.

Wilson, Jonathan. *Marc Chagall*. New York: Schocken, 2007.

ACKNOWLEDGMENTS

Many thanks to Katja Rivera, research associate,
Department of Modern and Contemporary Art at
the Art Institute of Chicago, for her knowledgeable
comments on Chagall's life, the text, and art.

TO MY MARC —B.R.

**FOR JULIA, MAY YOU ALWAYS KNOW
WHERE HOME IS —M.G.**

THIS IS A BORZOI BOOK PUBLISHED BY ALFRED A. KNOPF

Text copyright © 2018 by Barb Rosenstock
Jacket art and interior illustrations copyright © 2018 by Mary GrandPré

All rights reserved. Published in the United States by Alfred A. Knopf,
an imprint of Random House Children's Books, a division of Penguin
Random House LLC, New York.

Visit us on the Web! rhcbooks.com

Educators and librarians, for a variety of teaching tools, visit us at
RHTeachersLibrarians.com

Library of Congress Cataloging-in-Publication Data is available upon request.
ISBN 978-1-5247-1751-3 (trade) — ISBN 978-1-5247-1752-0 (lib. bdg.) —
ISBN 978-1-5247-1753-7 (ebook)

The text of this book is set in 16-point Old Style Goudy.
The display type is set in Neutraface 2 Display and MostraOne Regular.

The illustrations were created with acrylic paint on board.

MANUFACTURED IN CHINA
September 2018
10 9 8 7 6 5 4 3 2 1

First Edition